# Mother is heaven
## and
# Father is way to heaven

**Nadeem Pasha**

**BLUEROSE PUBLISHERS**
India | U.K.

Copyright © Nadeem Pasha 2025

All rights reserved by author. No part of this publication may be reproduced, stored in a retrieval system or transmitted in any form or by any means, electronic, mechanical, photocopying, recording or otherwise, without the prior permission of the author. Although every precaution has been taken to verify the accuracy of the information contained herein, the publisher assumes no responsibility for any errors or omissions. No liability is assumed for damages that may result from the use of information contained within.

BlueRose Publishers takes no responsibility for any damages, losses, or liabilities that may arise from the use or misuse of the information, products, or services provided in this publication.

For permissions requests or inquiries regarding this publication, please contact:

BLUEROSE PUBLISHERS
www.BlueRoseONE.com
info@bluerosepublishers.com
+91 8882 898 898
+4407342408967

ISBN: 978-93-6783-360-5

Cover design: Yash Singhal
Typesetting: Namrata Saini

First Edition: February 2025

Greetings!! When we came to this world, we could not talk, understand, walk, run, etc. But what we all do is cry, cry, and cry! And the first thing we see is our Mother. Who is all to us and understands everything about a child and all the needs even when we are unable to speak a single word. Mother is always helping with all my needs; when a child cries and when needed all the necessary medications. I love my mother, who is my world and my father, is the second person I saw, who cares for me, calls me many sweet names, kisses me, and sees me with lots of love and affection. It is almost as if he has achieved a big success in life that his family begins. And later we have seen many others' family members who are always caring and make me laugh, smile and celebrate my birthday with so much of happiness, gifts, cake and colorful decoration and when my parents took me outside, even on roads, supermarkets while walking, every one use to see me and smile and make faces so that I smile many times. when I was two years, old I see my mother always close to me. My dad was as well, but sometimes my father is not. However, I am happy with my mother, that there was someone who was always with me nurtured me, especially when I was sick and in need. Sometime when I was 4 years old and feeling sick suffering from fever, my parents became so restless and emotional. When doctor wants me to inject but even before I was injected my father is at medical store to buy needle and give it to doctor his heart was so heavy and his eyes was numb, but parents wants me to be healthy and happy as always I want to be means parents main targets is to see their kids always happy at any ages they pray every day to god to be healthy more than anything.

First day of School: My parents were so happy to admit me to the school and bring me books, a uniform, shoes and a school bag. I was happy too, looking at so many gifts, and then took a bath and got ready for school, with my parents both beaming till they had to drop me at the gate of school. when we entered the school gate for the first time, I was felt like crying and my heart was heavy. My loving parents were going far and far away, and I ran back to them crying, I don't want to go back to the class at the same time my mother cried turning her back towards me, but my Hero, my Father consoled me that they are just sitting outside the class until the lessons were over. My parents did not go home meanwhile I have a class teacher and I had new friends having fun, and later I was comfortable going to class alone now I know my parents will come to pick me up after school.

First Demand of Mine: I asked my father to get me a new cycle, and my father said he will get it for me soon but every day I used to ask him where is my cycle? He replied, "Very soon you will have it." Then I noticed my father wasnot coming home every night as he usually did. I demanded the answer form my mother, and asked if there was any issue with my him. my mother said my father is working overtime to arrange for the cycle as my father was working for a small company with an okay salary. One day he gifted me the Cycle I wanted, and I was so happy and my parent seeing that felt happy too. Soon after, I was told that I was going to have a sister to play with and then one day I found my sister in my mother's lap, and we always had a good time with family. When I was ten years old, I wanted to join the cricket camp, and I demanded it again for it; my father, then got me admitted as our financial conditions were becoming better and better. My father owned a 1bhk flat for us. Then I had been friending many friends, but one of my friends who was in 9th standard, and he did have father and his financial conditions were not good. One day, he said, "I want to buy some books." His mother was working in some Garment company as a helper. I told my father about my friend. He then sponsored him and guided me that we should always help people in need specially who are orphans. Then, I also realised that father is a god's gift and that having caring parents who are beside me for anything is an even greater blessing.

One day, I had guessed who my father's friend was. He was a good person, and he was always advancing me to study well and achieve my dreams, because I was dull in studies,focusing on my game and friends, and later my father advised me to even study well, but Studies and Skills are both as important as wings for any bird flying in the sky. My Cousin also stayed close to my house, and we always visited them and shared happiness but my cousin's family was not so happy.

As Uncle and Aunty always fought and both wanted to work, they wanted their kids to be taken care of by a housemaid. They had two kids: one was a six-month-old baby and the other an eight-year-old boy. My father always tells them that one person from the family itself should take care of the kids, yet they don't agree on this. One day I heard my dad saying to my uncle, "Why are you not satisfied with your earnings?" Since both of them had good salaries, but they had no peace in life, he remembered how his childhood days and his parents were very peaceful and had no worries. In the pursuit of a successful life, he left his parents behind. His father passed away before he got married, and after marriage, his wife said she didn't want to stay with her mother, as they had always had issues between them. Later, he asked his brothers and sisters to take care of their mother, but they said they also had problems in their lives. In the end, everyone decided to ask their mother to stay in an old age home so that they could visit and take care of her every day. At first, they visited her regularly, but soon they became too busy to visit her often. In the old age home, their mother would cry, saying, "A mother can grow and take care of many kids, but those kids can't take care of one mother." This was noticed by the manager of the old age home.

My uncle said his mother is in an old age home, and he hasn't visited her for a couple of months. He cried. My father then said to him to go meet her first, and soon after, the pandemic was announced. Everyone started working from home and was safeguarding their families first, rather than old parents they were about. Calling old parents over the phone, and they feel okay! We are done! Paid the share of the old age fee. I feel sad when I listen, and I pray to God that she should be happy and safe there. Later, my father and I used to go to the old age home just to see her, but we were not allowed inside due to pandemic rules. We later came to know that the management of the old age home was very good and they took care of the residents well, but loneliness still kills. Again, we tried to go and meet her, and this time we were able to see her. Upon seeing us, she cried and said that after a long time, she could finally see some relatives. We spent some time with her, and she told us that for the past 10 months, no one had come to visit her, aside from phone calls that lasted just two minutes. I asked a question to my dad: "Are you also like Uncle?" Why do people fail to love back parents as they always do? My father had tears in his eyes and said, "I am poor compared to others, but I have never let my parents down, and that's why we are happy and have no worries."

Later my father said, "I will tell you how I had life with my parents, but let me make Uncle's mother

(Aunty) feel better first," and my father said, "We are also a part of your family; please don't worry." My son and I will visit you always, and sometimes, with your permission, we will take you to our home. She felt so good and blessed us. Said, "Almighty, always keep you happy," my father said. These words and blessings won't go to waste, and this is real success.

# Why are we far from Success?

We are pushing for success, but we don't really know if this is the reason. We need success, but without the blessings from our elders, that is impossible. We have time for world tours and to visit many other dream places but no time to visit our own parents. You know what parents need in their last days? They need their loving family to stay close by. It's like their last wish, but they don't want to say it since you may feel pressured. But everyone has too many personal and other reasons. Still, you can make time to take them out to the park or the hospital and try to make them happy by spending time with them and keeping all your tension aside. Have you ever tried it? Try once and get their blessings; soon you will realize that you are closer to success. Remember their sacrifices when we were toddlers and had no sense of good or bad? They made us grow up clean, giving us healthy food and medication. They have not eaten in restaurants, they have stopped wearing branded clothes, they have stopped wearing jewelry, and they have stopped all the luxury to try to give us all good in return. What we give is pain? Pain, if we give them, can we live our life happily? We should ask this question to ourselves. See, nature will again bring you into its orbit. Now you are parents just starting your parenting journey, and you will also start to sacrifice and raise your kids to be a gentlemen. Again, you will be a kid, and your kids will be teaching you what is right and what is wrong. Now if you have not obeyed your parents, God will make your kids your masters, and they will teach and you will agree. What experiences do parents have in real life that their children coming from a generation of AI (Artificial Intelligence) where the real experiences of life people now browse, not live? Money is not everything, but it is necessary for life. I have seen many a case where people kill their own family for property, but one day we have to leave this world without anything, and at that time, if you remember, our names become body. The first thing that happens as soon as anyone dies is that his own name replaces the body. Name is what everyone wants in this world, for which money is needed more, rubbing humanity and more and not respecting parents and family. Now it's time to think about whether we are the right part of humanity.

The idea of success is subjective and often varies from one person to another. Some define it by material wealth, professional achievement, or personal growth, while others view it as a harmonious balance of all these factors. In many cultures, especially those with strong family values, the blessings of parents are considered an integral component of success. These blessings are often seen as the moral and spiritual foundation upon which success is built. However, modern society poses an interesting question: Can we still achieve success without the blessings of our parents? Is parental approval necessary for individual accomplishment, or can one chart their own path independently? This essay explores why some believe we are far from success without parental blessings and whether it is possible to attain success without them.

The Emotional and Psychological Significance of Parental Blessings Parents, in many cultures and communities, symbolize guidance, love, and moral support. From childhood, parents are often the first role models we encounter, shaping our values, principles, and understanding of the world. Their blessings are seen as expressions of their approval and confidence in their child's abilities. For many, this approval becomes an emotional anchor, providing a sense of stability and moral righteousness.

When parents offer their blessings, it can instill a profound sense of inner peace and self-assurance in their children. These feelings, in turn, nurture confidence, a key ingredient for success. For those who rely heavily on emotional support, parental blessings can function as an invaluable source of encouragement. The absence of this blessing may create emotional turmoil, insecurity, or even guilt, especially in cultures where parental respect is deeply ingrained. The fear of disappointing one's parents may hinder an individual's pursuit of their goals, potentially leading to a sense of failure or inadequacy.

Parental Blessings as a Cultural Expectation In many traditional societies, success is viewed not just as an individual achievement but also as a reflection of one's upbringing and familial relationships. Parents are seen as custodians of ancestral knowledge, values, and blessings, which are passed down through generations. Disobeying or disregarding one's parents may be perceived as a rejection of these values, distancing the individual from spiritual and cultural success.

In such contexts, parental blessings are not just an emotional or psychological need but a social expectation. The absence of parental approval may lead to societal judgment or exclusion, further alienating the individual from the community. This cultural narrative reinforces the idea that one cannot be truly successful unless they are in harmony with their family.

Breaking Away: Redefining Success in Modern Society

On the other hand, modern society has evolved to embrace individualism. Many people define success in terms of personal fulfillment, career growth, financial independence, or creative expression, rather than adherence to cultural or familial expectations. In this framework, success can be achieved without parental blessings, as the focus shifts from external approval to self-determination and autonomy.

For those who have difficult relationships with their parents or come from toxic family environments, seeking validation or blessings may not be feasible. In such cases, cutting ties or moving away from parental influence may be necessary for personal growth and mental well-being. The pursuit of success in this context is about finding inner strength, resilience, and self-actualization, independent of family approval.

Many successful individuals, whether in business, the arts, or other fields, have thrived without their parents' blessings or approval. By redefining success on their own terms, they break free from the constraints of traditional expectations, demonstrating that success can be achieved through perseverance, hard work, and self-belief.

## Can We Be Truly Successful Without Parental Blessings?

Whether or not we can be truly successful without parental blessings depends largely on how success is defined. If success is rooted in inner peace, fulfillment, and societal approval, then parental blessings may play a crucial role. However, if success is defined as personal achievement, growth, and independence, it is entirely possible to achieve it without parental involvement.

Success is deeply personal and multifaceted. While parental blessings can offer emotional and spiritual strength, they are not the only path to fulfillment. Ultimately, each individual must decide for themselves what success means and whether parental blessings are a necessary component of that journey. Those who find themselves far from their parents' approval can still carve out successful lives by focusing on their own values, dreams, and goals.

## Conclusion

Parental blessings are undoubtedly valuable for many people, offering emotional security, societal approval, and spiritual grounding. However, success without parental blessings is also increasingly common in not only possible but is a world where individualism is celebrated. People can and do achieve great things without the validation or approval of their parents, finding fulfillment through personal growth, resilience, and determination. Whether or not parental blessings are essential for success depends on the individual's values and the context in which they define success. Ultimately, true success comes from within, guided by one's own vision and inner strength.

## Are we on the right path for humanity?

We as humans take birth in this world through our parents, which means life takes place here. As parents, it is our duty to raise a good human being who society can see through their nature, good thoughts, and teachings. They should be like pure water flowing in a garden, so that everyone wants to drink from their clean and pure form. I have seen and heard about a few real humans who really make their actions a lesson to many. I have come across a case in the civil court where two elderly siblings were fighting for their parents. A younger put a case against the elder brother saying, "So many years my mother stayed in my brother's house; now I need my mother and it is my turn." At the same time, the elder brother said, "Oh God, bless me with good health to take care of my mother with my age and my weakness, instead of taking my mother away." How lucky is that mother whose kids are fighting for her? Wife and kids, at the same time, they are important; it is like a tree. The family tree is very much important. Parents are like roots; the husband is like the stem, branches are like sons, daughters, and in-laws, and the shadow is the wife who will keep the family safe from the heat. In the Society, most of the victims are elderly parents, which is why I have kept my strong feelings that there are few good people who support NGOs working to safeguard orphans, the elderly, women, children, and animals. Yes, this is humanity saving humanity. We have seen this more in the pandemic, where even family members did not come to claim their own family members helped them to get all the procedures done, especially doctors and so many real humans. They are the real heroes. I have noticed that saving someone's life makes you a hero in society, while when killing people, others for whatever reason, they can face their own family. Whenever they face others, people see them as like a zombie, and slowly cut off their relationships. Also, their family pays for their crime mentally.

It is important to watch all this that our growing generations is and the type of message being conveyed is wrong. Humanity is first, which will keep ourselves and society safe and happy. I still remember a video I saw on social media that showed how every single person kept helping one another, and it went on and on, making everyone feel happy. Even a small help to any person you have done that impacts a lot; he will make him respect you all the time. Even if he sees you on the way, he will have a smile on his face looking at you. The habit of helping each other is a good start to humanity. I teach my kids that if we are in traffic and there is an ambulance going by with its sirens on, or if it is in traffic, we should pray for them for a minute: "Oh God, please give him good health." Amen. Now my kids are always praying whenever they hear an ambulance. Now they know that we should respect all human beings. I remember my father saying to me that if you have money, then help the poor; if you are poor, then try to help them by sharing their pain and giving good advice, if you can, because many don't give good advice and some people don't even smile. We are very smart when we are in good times of life and want to become more successful, but when things are not working and when we feel low, we become fools and do nonsense.

## Are We on the Right Path of Humanity Without Respecting Our Parents?

Respect for parents has long been considered a cornerstone of moral behavior and a reflection of one's values. Across cultures and throughout history, the idea that honoring one's parents is fundamental to being a good human being has been deeply ingrained. This respect is not just about following societal norms, but is tied to the appreciation of the sacrifices, love, and guidance that parents often provide throughout their children's lives. In many religious, cultural, and philosophical traditions, respecting one's parents is seen as essential for personal development and ethical living. But in today's fast-paced, individualistic world, where modern values often clash with traditional ones, an important question arises: Can we be on the right path of humanity if we fail to respect our parents? This essay explores why respecting our parents is crucial for being a good human being and maintaining the moral fabric of society.

## The Importance of Parents in Shaping Humanity

Parents play a foundational role in the development of a child, not just biologically, but emotionally and ethically. They are typically the first people to instill values, teach empathy, and introduce concepts of right and wrong. In many ways, the moral compass we carry into adulthood is shaped by the lessons and guidance of our parents.

Respecting parents, therefore, is a form of gratitude for their role in nurturing, protecting, and educating us. When we fail to honor them, we undermine the very foundation of our ethical understanding. Disrespecting parents can erode the sense of duty, compassion, and responsibility that is central to what it means to be a good human being.

In cultures around the world, filial piety—respect for one's parents and ancestors—is regarded as one of the highest virtues. This respect is not just about obedience but involves honoring their wisdom, understanding their sacrifices, and recognizing the role they played in our growth. Without this fundamental respect, we may stray from the path of humanity, as the lessons they imparted often lay the groundwork for how we treat others in society.

## **The Role of Respect in Building Character**

A key argument for why we cannot be on the right path of humanity without respecting our parents lies in the way respect builds character. When we respect our parents, we learn humility, patience, empathy, and compassion. These qualities are essential for being a good human being. They teach us to understand the perspectives of others, to show gratitude for the efforts made on our behalf, and to value relationships.

Respecting our parents is not always easy, especially in moments of disagreement or generational conflict. However, the ability to respect them despite differences is a mark of maturity and ethical growth. It demonstrates our ability to rise above personal frustrations and recognize the importance of family and community. If we cannot show respect to the very people who gave us life, how can we expect to show it to others in broader society?

The lack of respect for parents often reflects a larger issue of self-centeredness, which is increasingly prevalent in today's world. In our pursuit of personal success, independence, and individuality, many may forget the importance of respecting the people and individuals who laid the foundation for that success. This disregard can lead to a more selfish society, where personal desires take precedence over communal and familial bonds, steering us away from the right path of humanity.

## The Intergenerational Bond and Its Ethical Implications

The relationship between parents and children is more than just a familial connection; it represents the transmission of values, culture, and wisdom across generations. By respecting our parents, we ensure the continuation of this intergenerational bond. Parents, in turn, pass on lessons that were taught to them by their own parents, creating a cycle of moral and ethical knowledge that benefits society as a whole.

Disrespecting this bond not only harms the individual but weakens the moral fabric of society. When younger generations fail to respect their elders, they disrupt this cycle of learning and moral guidance. A society that dismisses the value of elders, risks losing its sense of history, wisdom, and ethical continuity.

In many traditional societies, elders are seen as the keepers of wisdom and experience, and their guidance is essential for younger generations to navigate life's challenges. Respecting parents, therefore, is not just about personal morality; it is about maintaining a connection with the past and preserving the ethical principles that sustain human communities.

## Can We Be Good Human Beings Without Respecting Our Parents?

At the core of the question lies a broader issue: What does it mean to be a good human being? While respecting parents is certainly a vital component of ethical living, being a good human being encompasses a wide range of virtues, including kindness, honesty, empathy, and respect for others. However, respect for parents is often the starting point for developing these virtues. If we fail to respect the people who have sacrificed the most for us, how can we cultivate these other virtues in a meaningful way? Without respect for parents, we risk becoming detached from the values that shape us as moral individuals. Moreover, disrespecting our parents can lead to strained relationships, emotional pain, and a lack of personal fulfilment, all of which can detract from our ability to live meaningful, compassionate lives.

While it is possible to be kind, successful, or even socially conscious without having a good relationship with one's parents, the lack of respect for them may suggest an incomplete understanding of what it means to truly care for others. A person who fails to honor their parents may struggle to show respect to others, as the principles of empathy, compassion, and responsibility begin at home.

## Conclusion

Respecting our parents is more than a cultural expectation; it is a fundamental component of what it means to be a good human being. Parents are the first people who teach us how to navigate the world, offering lessons in morality, empathy, and responsibility. By respecting them, we honor the role they have played in shaping our lives and demonstrate the kind of compassion and humility necessary for a humane society.

Without this respect, we risk losing our connection to the values that guide ethical behavior and the wisdom passed down through generations. While being a good human being encompasses a range of virtues, respect for our parents lays the foundation for the development of these qualities. Therefore, to walk the right path of humanity, we must ensure that we honor and respect those who have played a central role in our moral and personal growth.

# People are Smart but Sometimes a Fool

I came across news in a paper that a family died after consuming poison—parents and two kids. Neighbors said that they had loans and some people were treating them very badly since he was a defaulter. One defaulter, but the entire family suffers. Take wise decisions before you act because if he had taken a small loan and slowly reached success, then he and his family would have sustained because Patience is Life. We can't save them, but we can help people who are still facing such situations. The first thing is to know that we should have strong patience when facing such issues. We have created the issue by taking loans, and we should work to clear the loans over time according to our earning limits. First, go to the police; they can assist you and take legal advice. Share your feelings with family members, and trust that soon help is coming from God. Many take loans unnecessarily just because they are expecting some money to come in the future, and later, when they do not get it, they struggle to repay the loan. Now the situation is for him like: Why did I not stop myself? (See the importance of Patience) Begin; non-patience is (trapped) life is hell now.

When we are in good times of life, we should also expect that bad times may come, because they will come after a day. Being safe is important, even when you are sitting in a dora-dora. Driving a car requires using a seatbelt to save lives. All this is an example of don't be impatient. I have seen many take out big home loans and later become defaulters, losing their confidence and taking bad steps, becoming fools. See and learn from birds. They also make homes (nests) with lots of effort and lay eggs, safeguarding them. When there is rain or wind, and their nests fall down, they trust in God and make another one later. We need to plan accordingly as per our requirements and also stop unnecessary spending.

People Are Smart but Sometimes Foolish: The Tragic Choice of Ignoring Our Parents

In today's fast-paced, modern world, people often pride themselves on being intelligent, independent, and capable of making their own decisions. This self-confidence, while empowering, can sometimes lead to unintended consequences—especially when it comes to how we treat our parents. It is a painful irony that while we consider ourselves smart and progressive, we sometimes make foolish choices regarding those who raised us. One such choice is the decision to ignore the feelings and needs of our parents, often leading to the heart-wrenching act of sending them to old age homes without truly considering what they feel or need.

As we grow older, many of us get wrapped up in our own lives—careers, families, and personal ambitions. In the process, we often fail to understand that our parents, who once devoted their lives to our upbringing, now seek companionship, care, and love from us in their later years. Yet, in many cases, we neglect their emotional needs. We may convince ourselves that old age homes are the best option for them, rationalizing that they will receive professional care or be with others their age. While there may be practical reasons for this decision, it's often a reflection of our desire for convenience rather than what is truly best for them.

What we fail to consider is the deep emotional pain and loneliness many parents feel when asked to move to an old age home. They may feel abandoned, as though they are no longer important in their children's lives. After years of sacrifice and hard work to ensure a better future for their children, they find themselves pushed away from the very family they helped build. The pain of being sent to an old age home often lies not in the facility itself, but in the knowledge that their own children—their pride and joy—have chosen to separate them from the family unit.

The emotional burden of this decision is something many of us, in our "smart" decision-making, fail to truly understand. It can be easy to overlook the unspoken longing our parents have for connection, the desire to stay involved in our lives, and the need to feel loved and valued. In their later years, what they crave most is not luxury or professional care but the simple act of being with family—feeling the warmth and love of their children and grandchildren.

While we may be smart in many ways—successful in our careers, well-educated, and progressive in our thinking—our inability to truly empathize with our parents in these moments reveals a blind spot in our understanding. We become foolish in our pursuit of what we think is "best," ignoring the emotional and psychological needs of the very people who once sacrificed their own needs for us.

True wisdom comes not just from making logical decisions but from balancing logic with empathy, understanding, and respect for our elders. Instead of sidelining our parents and considering old age homes as the easy solution, we should be asking ourselves how we can create an environment where they feel loved, cared for, and part of the family. They need our time, attention, and companionship far more than anything else.

In ignoring their feelings, we may be missing out on the deeper connection that comes from honoring and caring for those who raised us. People are smart, but sometimes, in moments like these, we are also fools.

When we are parents, are we making our kids good humans?

Parenting is one of the most significant responsibilities in life, and the way we raise our children shapes the kind of adults they become. A crucial question that every parent must ask themselves is whether they are fostering values that encourage their children to grow into compassionate, responsible, and kind individuals. Being a good human entails empathy, respect, integrity, and the ability to think beyond oneself. To instill these qualities in children, it is essential to lead by example. When parents demonstrate kindness in their daily lives, children learn to mirror this behavior. Whether it's through small acts of generosity or showing respect to others, children absorb these values as part of their own.

One of the core aspects of raising good humans is teaching respect—both for family and for others. Respect starts at home, where children learn the dynamics of relationships. Parents need to create an environment where mutual respect is practiced. This involves not only disciplining children when they cross boundaries but also showing them respect by listening to their opinions, acknowledging their emotions, and treating them as individuals with their own thoughts and feelings. Establishing clear family values, encouraging open communication, and showing unconditional-love all contribute to fostering respect for family and parents.

To help children become good humans and cultivate respect, parents must also provide consistent guidance and support. Teaching the importance of family ties can be done through quality time spent together, celebrating traditions, and highlighting the significance of family during tough times. Encouraging responsibility from a young age, such as assigning small chores or asking children to help with family decisions, fosters a sense of belonging and accountability. By doing this, children not only learn to value their parents but also come to understand the broader concept of respect and compassion toward others, leading them to grow into well-rounded, respectful adults.

As we navigate through life, the way we treat our parents has a direct influence not only on our current relationships but also on how our children will one day treat us. Our actions, attitudes, and values serve as silent lessons to the next generation, shaping their understanding of what it means to be a good human being. When we ignore or neglect our parents, fail to show them respect, or even send them to old age homes without considering their emotional needs, we risk passing down these behaviors to our children. The question that arises is: Are we setting the right example for our children and raising them to be good human beings?

**Children Learn by Example**

Children are highly observant, and they learn most of their life lessons not from what we tell them, but from what we do. The way we treat our parents forms a template for how our children will treat us in the future. If they see us being neglectful or indifferent towards our aging parents, they may internalize the idea that this behavior is acceptable. We may unknowingly be teaching them that once someone becomes old, they are a burden to be managed rather than a loved one to be cherished.

This cycle of behavior can perpetuate itself across generations. By being disobedient or disrespectful toward our parents, we are laying the groundwork for our own future, where our children may treat us in similar ways. If we fail to show compassion and care to our parents, our children may grow up lacking those same values, becoming disconnected from the very essence of what it means to be a good human being—showing kindness, empathy, and respect to others, especially the elderly.

## The Importance of Teaching Respect for Elders

Respect for elders, especially parents, is a fundamental value that helps shape the moral and emotional development of a child. It is through observing how we treat our parents that children learn the importance of family bonds, loyalty, and responsibility. When we, as parents, fail to honor and respect our own parents, we risk raising children who may become self-centered, detached, and dismissive of the importance of family.

By being respectful, attentive, and loving toward our parents, we teach our children the values of compassion, responsibility, and gratitude. These values are essential to raising good human beings—individuals who are not only successful in life but who also have the capacity to care for others, be kind, and contribute positively to society.

## The Future Consequences of Neglect

When children witness their parents neglecting or disregarding the emotional needs of their grandparents, they may grow up with a distorted view of how to handle relationships, particularly with aging family members. They may see the elderly as a burden, or worse, something to discard when inconvenient. This attitude leads to a breakdown of family structures and weakens the bonds that keep generations connected. If we expect our children to care for us with love and respect in the future, it is crucial that we model this behavior now with our own parents.

Neglecting our parents and sending them to old age homes without truly considering their needs and emotions sends a strong message to our children that such behavior is permissible. Later, when we are old and dependent on our children for support, we may find that they, too, follow this pattern of neglect. The hurt and loneliness we inflict on our parents today may become the very same pain we experience in the future.

**Creating a Legacy of Love and Care**

Being a good parent goes beyond providing for the physical and educational needs of our children. It involves instilling in them the values that make them empathetic and compassionate human beings. To raise good humans, we need to demonstrate what it means to respect, honor, and care for those who raised us. This means being patient with our parents, listening to their needs, and ensuring they feel loved and valued, even in their old age.

By treating our parents with dignity and care, we set a powerful example for our children. We teach them that family is not a disposable unit, but a lifelong bond that must be nurtured with love, respect, and responsibility. This is how we create a legacy of kindness that can carry forward into the future, ensuring that our children grow up to become good human beings who treat others with the same respect and love they witnessed in their own family.

**Conclusion**

When we become parents, our actions speak louder than words. The way we treat our parents today will echo in how our children treat us tomorrow. If we are disobedient, neglectful, or dismissive of our aging parents, we run the risk of passing down these behaviors to the next generation. In contrast, by showing love, respect, and compassion toward our parents, we raise children who value family bonds and understand the importance of being good human beings. As parents, it is our responsibility not only to provide for our children but also to model the values that will help them grow into caring, empathetic, and responsible adults.

# Mother is Always Praised but Father is Always Fulfilling Our Demands

Mothers are often revered as symbols of love, sacrifice, and nurturing. Their role in a child's life is frequently praised, highlighting their tenderness and emotional support. From the moment a child is born, the mother is viewed as the primary caregiver, the one who provides constant affection and guidance. Society glorifies her for the countless hours spent caring for her family, making her a figure of unconditional love and emotional strength. Her influence is seen in the gentle lessons she imparts about empathy, patience, and resilience.

Fathers, on the other hand, are often seen through a more practical lens. While the father's emotional support is equally important, his role is frequently overshadowed by his contributions as a provider. He is expected to fulfill the material needs of the family, ensuring their financial security and stability. The societal image of a father is often associated with meeting demands — whether it's paying for education, buying things the family needs, or working tirelessly to ensure a better future. His sacrifices are sometimes less visible, but they are no less significant.

This disparity in how mothers and fathers are perceived can sometimes lead to the underappreciation of the father's role. A father's love is expressed in ways that are different, often quieter and more pragmatic. His presence may not always be defined by affection in the same way as the mothers, but his actions speak volumes about his dedication to his family's well-being.

Society, however, tends to focus more on the father's role as a provider rather than acknowledging the emotional support and love he offers, which can go unnoticed.

In reality, both parents play crucial roles in shaping a child's life, each contributing uniquely. While the mother is praised for her nurturing, the father's commitment to fulfilling the family's needs is equally an expression of his deep love. It is important to recognize that both emotional and material contributions are valuable and vital for the holistic development of children. Both parents deserve equal recognition and appreciation for their sacrifices, efforts, and love.

In many societies, mothers are celebrated and revered for their nurturing and caring roles. They are praised for their unconditional love, emotional warmth, and for being the backbone of the family. However, while mothers receive recognition for their sacrifices, fathers often play a more understated role, fulfilling their children's demands, providing for the family, and offering stability and security. Yet, despite their significant contributions, fathers frequently go unappreciated, and the respect they deserve is often overshadowed by the visible care associated with mothers. This imbalance is not only unfair but also perpetuates the misconception that fathers are solely providers, when in reality, they play a crucial role in their children's emotional and personal development as well.

## The Role of the Father: More Than a Provider

For generations, the role of the father has been traditionally viewed as the breadwinner—the one who works tirelessly to meet the financial needs of the family. This role, while vital, often places fathers in the background of family life, making their contributions seem less visible compared to the nurturing role of mothers. Fathers, however, do much more than just fulfill financial demands. They provide structure, guidance, discipline, and emotional support in ways that are less acknowledged.

Many fathers work long hours or take on challenging jobs to ensure that their children have access to education, opportunities, and a comfortable lifestyle. While mothers may receive recognition for being emotionally present, fathers often provide a sense of security through their hard work and perseverance. They may not always express their emotions as openly as mothers do, but this does not diminish the depth of their love and dedication to their family. Their sacrifices are often silent, yet they are just as significant.

## The Emotional Bond Between Fathers and Children

Although traditionally viewed as the less expressive parent, fathers play a crucial role in the emotional development of their children. A father's love, guidance, and encouragement help build a child's self-confidence, emotional strength, and sense of identity. Fathers often teach their children important life lessons—how to face challenges, how to work hard, and how to remain resilient in the face of adversity. These lessons are invaluable in shaping a child's character and future success.

Despite this, fathers are often taken for granted, and their emotional contributions can be overlooked. Society tends to praise mothers for their warmth and care while underestimating the nurturing role of fathers. This imbalance creates a situation where fathers are often viewed as the "fixers" or the ones to turn to for financial or practical needs, but not necessarily for emotional support. This can lead to a lack of respect for fathers, despite the significant role they play in their children's lives.

## The Unrecognized Sacrifices of Father

Fathers make many sacrifices that often go unnoticed. In the pursuit of providing for their families, they may work long hours, take on stressful jobs, or even forego personal dreams and ambitions to ensure that their children have everything they need. These sacrifices are sometimes dismissed as just "doing their job," but in reality, they are acts of love and devotion that deserve recognition and respect.

Fathers often face societal pressure to be the strong, silent providers, expected to manage stress without complaint and handle family responsibilities without asking for acknowledgment. This expectation can sometimes make it difficult for fathers to express their emotional needs or to feel appreciated for their efforts. Over time, this lack of appreciation can lead to feelings of frustration or sadness, as they may feel undervalued in their role.

While mothers often receive vocal praise and acknowledgment for their role in the family, fathers rarely receive the same level of emotional recognition. Their sacrifices—working tirelessly, providing for the family, being there when needed—are often seen as obligations rather than choices made out of love and commitment. This unfair perception can create a disconnect, where fathers are left feeling unappreciated despite their essential role in the family.

## The Need for Equal Recognition and Respect

The truth is, both parents play equally important roles in the lives of their children, and both deserve respect, acknowledgment, and appreciation. While mothers are praised for their nurturing qualities, fathers should also be respected for the stability, guidance, and protection they provide. They are not just there to fill financial or material needs, but are pillars of emotional support, role models, and mentors for their children.

Fathers deserve to be appreciated for more than just their ability to fulfill demands. Their love, though often expressed through action rather than words, is just as deep and meaningful as a mother's. Fathers who sacrifice their time, energy, and dreams for their children should be honored and respected for their selflessness. They deserve more than just a nod of acknowledgment for "doing their job"; they deserve genuine recognition for their integral role in shaping their children's lives.

By offering fathers the same respect and admiration that we often give to mothers, we create a more balanced understanding of the family unit. Both parents contribute in unique and essential ways, and both are deserving of love, praise, and gratitude. Children who grow up respecting both their parents equally are more likely to understand the importance of partnership, balance, and shared responsibility in life.

**Conclusion**

While mothers are rightly praised for their nurturing and caregiving roles, fathers often remain in the background, quietly fulfilling demands and providing for the family. Yet, this does not mean they are any less deserving of respect. Fathers make countless sacrifices, offer emotional support, and play a critical role in their children's development, even if their contributions are less visible. It is important to acknowledge and respect fathers for all that they do, recognizing that their role in the family is just as valuable and significant as that of mothers. Only when we truly appreciate the contributions of both parents can we foster an environment of mutual respect, love, and balance within the family.

## What is the status of father and his sacrifices?

The status of a father in a family is often defined by his unwavering commitment to ensuring the happiness and well-being of his loved ones. Fathers traditionally assume the role of protectors and providers, often going to great lengths to offer stability and security. Whether it's working long hours or making personal sacrifices, a father's efforts are focused on giving his family the best possible life. His presence is a quiet assurance that the family's needs will be met, even if his contributions are not always immediately recognized or celebrated.

One of the greatest sacrifices fathers make is the time they give up to provide for their families. While balancing work and family life, they often miss out on key moments with their children in their pursuit of financial security and comfort for the household. This sacrifice, though not always visible, is done out of love and a desire to ensure a bright future for their children. Fathers often prioritize the needs of their family above their personal dreams, ambitions, and even health, highlighting the depth of their selflessness.

Beyond financial contributions, fathers also provide emotional strength and guidance, even if they don't always express their feelings as openly as mothers. A father sacrifices often include setting aside his own stress, challenges, or desires to be a stable and reliable figure for his family. He silently bears the weight of responsibility, ensuring that his family can pursue happiness and growth without being burdened by the difficulties he faces. In many ways, this unseen emotional sacrifice is a testament to his deep love and devotion.

Ultimately, the father's sacrifices, whether visible or hidden, are a crucial foundation for a family's happiness. His efforts, often understated, create an environment where his children and spouse can thrive. Despite the lack of overt praise that fathers sometimes receive, their status within the family is indispensable. They quietly work behind the scenes to ensure that their loved ones have everything they need to lead fulfilling, happy lives. Recognizing the depth of a father's sacrifices helps us appreciate the true value of his contributions to the family's success and joy.

# When Parents Are Old Are We Responsible Towards Parents

Once upon a time, in a small village, there lived a man named Raj with his wife, Meera, and two children, Arjun and Aarti. Raj had worked tirelessly his entire life, ensuring his children had the best opportunities and a comfortable life. His wife, Meera, stood by his side, nurturing the family with love and care. As the years passed, Arjun and Aarti grew up and moved to the city for better prospects, leaving Raj and Meera behind in their old home.

Raj and Meera were proud of their children's accomplishments, but as they grew older, their health began to decline. Raj's strength was fading, and Meera's memory had started to falter. They still lived in the same home they had built with love, but their needs were now different. The once vibrant couple now required help for basic tasks and longed for the company of their children, who were busy with their own lives in the city. Arjun and Aarti would visit occasionally, but their visits grew fewer as their own responsibilities multiplied.

One day, Raj fell seriously ill, and Meera struggled to take care of him alone. Desperate, she called Arjun and Aarti for help. When they arrived, they saw the frail condition of their parents, realizing how much they had neglected them. Guilt weighed heavily on their hearts. The siblings sat down and had a heartfelt conversation, remembering all the sacrifices their parents had made for them. They realized that while they had been focused on their own lives, they had overlooked the most important responsibility — caring for their aging parents with love and affection.

Moved by this realization, Arjun and Aarti decided to make amends. They rearranged their lives to ensure that they could be there for their parents in their old age, just as Raj and Meera had always been there for them. They provided not just physical care but also emotional support, spending quality time with them, sharing stories, and laughing together like they used to. The love and affection they gave brought joy and comfort to their aging parents, proving that it was not just a responsibility, but a privilege to care for those who had devoted their lives to them. Through this experience, they learned that parents deserve the same love and attention in their old age that they once gave so selflessly.

# What Parents Expect from us in Old Age

As parents grow older, their expectations from their children shift from material support to emotional care and companionship. In their youth, parents often prioritize their children's happiness, sacrificing their own needs to ensure a bright future for their family. But as they age, their hopes become simpler. What parents seek most in their old age is the warmth of love, respect, and the reassurance that their children still cherish the bond they once nurtured. They long for companionship, a comforting presence in their lives, and a sense of belonging within the family they dedicated their lives to.

The greatest expectation parents have in their old age is to feel valued and appreciated. Having devoted countless years to raising their children, they hope that their efforts are not forgotten, and that their children will honor their sacrifices by showing them kindness and respect. Small gestures, like listening to their stories, spending time with them, or even a phone call, make a world of difference. They want to know that, even though their roles have changed, they are still an important part of their children's lives. For aging parents, the fear of being left behind or forgotten is profound, and they look to their children for reassurance that they still matter.

Physical support also becomes a key expectation as parents face the challenges of aging. They may no longer be able to manage the day-to-day tasks that were once second nature to them. In these moments, parents hope their children will step in with patience and understanding. Whether it's helping with chores, attending medical appointments, or just being there during difficult times, parents expect their children to be a source of strength and support. This is not just a practical need, but an emotional one — it is in these acts of care that parents feel the love and protection they once offered their children being returned to them.

Ultimately, what parents truly desire is to age with dignity and love. They do not expect grand gestures or luxurious gifts; what they need most is emotional closeness, a feeling that their children are still connected to them. The bond between parent and child is one of the strongest and most profound relationships, and in their old age, parents hope that this bond remains intact. As they grow older, they seek not just care, but genuine affection, empathy, and the security that comes from knowing that their children will always be there for them, just as they were in their children's early years.

Are we good humans? No, if we don't respect our own parents always.

Respect is one of the core values that define a person's character, and without it, we cannot truly call ourselves good humans. Respect goes beyond just words; it's about how we treat others, especially those who have played crucial roles in shaping our lives. It encompasses kindness, empathy, and understanding. Without respect, relationships lose their value, and we fail to recognize the dignity and worth of the people around us. At the heart of every relationship, especially with our parents, lies the fundamental need for respect. Without it, we become disconnected from the essence of what it means to be human.

Parents are often regarded as God's most precious gift, for they are the ones who guide us through life with unconditional love and sacrifice. From the moment we are born, they devote themselves to our well-being, often putting our needs ahead of their own. This makes them deserving of the highest respect. To honor our parents is to acknowledge their role in our lives and to show gratitude for the countless sacrifices they have made. By respecting them, we recognize the immense value they hold, not just as caretakers but as individuals who have shaped us into who we are.

Without respecting our parents, we risk losing sight of the deep bond that exists between parent and child. Disrespecting them is a betrayal of the love and care they have given us. It is not just an act of ingratitude but also a reflection of our own shortcomings as human beings. A good human recognizes the importance of honoring those who have played an essential role in their life, particularly their parents, who embody the most selfless form of love. Respecting them is a fundamental moral obligation that speaks to our character and humanity.

In essence, respect is the foundation of a meaningful and fulfilling life. To be good humans, we must show respect to those who have been a part of our journey, especially our parents, who are truly a divine gift. When we treat them with the love, dignity, and reverence they deserve, we not only become better individuals but also honor the divine nature of the parent-child relationship. Through respect, we acknowledge the profound role they play in our lives and embody the true essence of goodness, love, and humanity.

# Parents In Life and After Life (Valuable Than Any Other Thing)

Parents hold a unique and irreplaceable position in our lives, one that transcends time, circumstances, and even life itself. From the moment we are born, our parents become our first guides, protectors, and nurturers. Their love is unconditional, rooted in the very act of bringing us into this world and raising us. Regardless of how life evolves, this bond remains steadfast. While relationships with friends, colleagues, and even life partners may change over time, the connection with our parents endures. They are our foundation, shaping our early experiences, values, and sense of self.

Life partners, on the other hand, while deeply significant, are relationships that can be more fluid. In today's world, we have seen many instances where marriages end in divorce, and people move on to new relationships. However, the bond with our parents is different. It does not end when challenges arise, and even if we grow distant or experience conflict, the parent-child relationship remains an inherent part of who we are. We may see cases where individuals estrange themselves from their parents or even legally disown them, but emotionally, the impact of that relationship persists. Parents, even when hurt, often continue to care, hoping for reconciliation.

The permanence of parental love is such that it remains whether we are good to them or not. Parents continue to love and worry about their children, even when those children may not treat them well. This selfless love is what makes the parent-child bond so special. While a life partner may come and go based on compatibility and circumstances, parents are tied to us by something deeper—biology, history, and the formative experiences of our lives. Their love often remains unwavering, whether we succeed or fail, whether we are kind or indifferent.

Even after life, the influence of parents continues. Their teachings, their love, and their sacrifices leave a lasting legacy in our hearts and memories. Though life partners may change, and relationships with them may come and go, the role of parents in our lives is eternal. Whether we treat them with respect and care, or neglect them, parents remain an inseparable part of who we are. They are the constants in our lives, a gift that transcends time and circumstance, shaping us long after they are gone.

Did we understand parents? think by yourself and answer yourself.

Did we truly understand our parents? It's a big question, one that often goes unanswered until it's too late. As children, we grow up seeing our parents through a lens of expectation, sometimes assuming they exist solely to meet our needs and fulfill our desires. We may not realize the depth of their struggles, the sacrifices they silently make, or the dreams they set aside for our sake.

We often overlook their humanity, seeing them only as providers or caregivers, not as individuals with their own emotions, fears, and hopes. It's only later in life, when we face our own challenges, that we begin to see them more clearly. We start to understand the weight they carried, the patience they showed, and the love that ran deeper than we ever realized. The question, "Did we understand them?" "lingers, reminding us that perhaps we could have done more to appreciate them, to listen more carefully, and to love more openly.

# About the Author

Nadeem Pasha was born and raised in the bustling city of Bangalore. His childhood was full of memories of laughter and love, surrounded by his parents and nine siblings in a humble yet warm home. His father, a hardworking man, had always ensured that his large family was provided for, while his mother, a gentle and nurturing soul, dedicated her life to raising her children with love and care. They lived modestly, but their hearts were full of joy, and the bond between them seemed unbreakable.

However, as time passed, the inevitable came. When Nadeem's father passed away, the foundation of their family began to shake. The siblings who were once close-knit started to drift apart as they married, moved away, and began their own lives. Nadeem's mother, now a widow, was left with him. While all of her other children had their own commitments and families, it was Nadeem who stayed by her side. He watched as, one by one, his siblings distanced themselves, busy with their own lives, barely making time for the woman who had given them everything.

Years passed, and Nadeem's mother grew older, frailer, and lonelier. Now over 80 years old, she had become too weak to care for herself. Her heart still ached for all her children, but despite her constant worry and longing, none of them answered her calls or came to visit. Nadeem, too, had his own share of burdens. He had a wife who suffered from chronic health issues and three children who depended on him. Yet, despite the challenges, he could not abandon the woman who had sacrificed her entire life for her children.

Night after night, Nadeem sat by his mother's bedside as she lay awake, worrying about her other children. Her mind was consumed with thoughts of them, wondering why they hadn't called or come to see her. Though she longed for the love and attention of all her children, it was Nadeem who cared for her with unwavering devotion. He stayed up with her during sleepless nights, brought her food, and made sure she was never alone. While his siblings had their own commitments, Nadeem never saw his mother as a burden. To him, she was still the woman who had nurtured him, and he couldn't bear to see her forgotten by the very family she had built with love.

Despite the heavy burden Nadeem Pasha carried, he was not alone in his journey. His wife, though struggling with her own health issues, was a constant pillar of support. She understood the deep bond Nadeem shared with his mother and never once complained about the extra responsibility placed on their family. Despite her own pain, she found the strength to care for Nadeem's mother, cooking meals, helping with household chores, and even sitting with Nadeem's mother during her anxious, sleepless nights.

She never saw her mother-in-law as a burden, but rather as a part of the family that needed love and care.

Nadeem wife also never harbored any negative feelings toward the situation, despite the strain it placed on her own health and their family life. She understood how much Nadeem's mother meant to him, and she knew that caring for her was a reflection of the values they both held dear — love, respect, and duty towards their elders. She often reminded Nadeem of how fortunate they were to still have his mother with them, choosing to see the situation as an opportunity to honor and give back to the woman who had raised him. Her quiet resilience and positivity created an atmosphere of love and patience in their home, allowing Nadeem to continue his care without feeling overwhelmed.

Even though Nadeem's mother could see how difficult things were for the family, she never let herself be consumed by guilt or negativity. Instead, she found solace in the love Nadeem and his wife showed her, even as her heart still longed for the other children who had grown distant. She appreciated every small gesture, whether it was Nadeem sitting by her side, his wife making her a comforting meal, or their children checking in on her. She never expressed bitterness toward her other children, choosing instead to keep them in her prayers, hoping that one day they would return.

Through the hardships, Nadeem's household remained one filled with compassion and love. Though the weight of responsibility was heavy, Nadeem and his wife found strength in each other and in their shared values. Together, they ensured that Nadeem's mother lived her final years with dignity, surrounded by love, and without ever feeling abandoned or neglected. The true gift in their family was not the ease of life but the quiet strength and unwavering commitment that kept them bonded through even the most trying times.

Moral of the story : Parents Feelings are most important subject.

If everyone took the time to care for their parents, life would undoubtedly resemble a heavenly existence filled with love, respect, and gratitude. Each act of kindness toward our parents—whether it's simply spending time with them, listening to their stories, or providing the support they need—creates a ripple effect of joy and fulfillment within families. When we honor and care for those who brought us into this world, we foster an environment where compassion thrives, strengthening the bonds that unite us. In such a world, the worries and loneliness that often accompany old age would diminish, replaced by the warmth of family connections and mutual respect. Not only would our parents feel cherished and valued, but we too would experience the profound joy that comes from giving back to those who have sacrificed so much for our happiness. Ultimately, a society that prioritizes the care of its elders is one that nurtures its future, creating a cycle of love and support that transcends generations. So our upcoming generations respect us same way when we need them.

Respect Your Wife and Children: Fulfilling Their Needs While Setting an Example of Goodness and humanity.Respect, love, and support are the pillars of a healthy and happy family. As a husband and father, fulfilling the needs of your wife and children, while simultaneously respecting them, is not only a moral obligation but a reflection of your character. When a man shows respect to his family and leads by example, he becomes a powerful role model for his children, shaping their values and attitudes for life. This dynamic can create a positive ripple effect, allowing them to grow into good, humble, and respectful individuals who contribute to society and, in turn, receive the respect they deserve. By living a life rooted in humility and respect, a man can set the foundation for a family that embodies these qualities, thereby creating a chain of goodness that can impact the world for generations.

## The Importance of Respecting Your Wife and Children

Respecting your wife is more than just fulfilling her material needs; it's about treating her with dignity, appreciating her contributions to the family, and acknowledging her individuality. A respectful husband recognizes that marriage is a partnership, where both partners bring their unique strengths, and these should be honored. When a man respects his wife, he models a healthy, loving relationship for his children. His children learn that respect, communication, and equality are essential elements of a happy family life.

Respect for children, meanwhile, goes beyond providing for their physical well-being. It's about listening to them, valuing their opinions, and encouraging them to express themselves freely. When children are treated with respect, they develop confidence, a strong sense of self-worth, and learn how to respect others in return. By showing love, patience, and understanding, a father teaches his children the importance of treating people with kindness and empathy.

## Fulfilling Needs: Emotional and Material

It is important to fulfill the emotional and material needs of both your wife and children. While material provisions, such as ensuring they have food, clothing, shelter, and education, are essential, emotional needs are equally significant. Your wife needs to feel valued, supported, and loved, while your children need to feel secure, cared for, and understood.

Meeting emotional needs requires time, attention, and genuine interest in the well-being of your family members. Spending quality time with your wife and children, engaging in meaningful conversations, and being present during moments of joy and difficulty shows that you care about their happiness and well-being. By doing this, you create a loving and supportive environment that fosters emotional growth and strengthens family bonds.

Moreover, when a father treats his wife with respect, children learn that a healthy relationship involves mutual.

## The Importance of Family Over Money

Family is often regarded as the cornerstone of human existence, a bond that transcends all material wealth and success. While money is undeniably essential for survival in the modern world, it is ultimately a tool—one that provides comfort, security, and access to various resources. However, it lacks the emotional, psychological, and moral depth that family offers. In times of need, especially when life becomes challenging, family serves as the ultimate source of support, care, and unconditional love. This essay will explore the ways in which family is more important than money, emphasizing how a caring family remains with you through thick and thin, offering a kind of wealth that money can never replicate.

## 1. Emotional Support

Money may buy material comforts, but it cannot buy genuine emotional support. When life throws difficult situations—be it illness, loss, or stress—having a caring family by your side is invaluable. The power of a listening ear, a comforting hug, or a supportive conversation cannot be measured in monetary terms. A loving family offers stability and reassurance that no amount of wealth can provide. Emotional well-being is key to a happy life, and families play a vital role in fostering this through love, encouragement, and understanding.

In difficult times, it is often the family that provides solace. Whether it's grieving the loss of a loved one, going through a financial setback, or navigating a major life transition, the presence of family eases the burden. They remind you that you are not alone, that there are people who care deeply about you, regardless of your financial status. A family is a constant in life's ups and downs, offering an emotional safety net when the world feels harsh and uncaring.

## 2. Unconditional Love

Money can create transactional relationships, where people might care about you for what you can offer them materially. However, family relationships, particularly in a healthy and caring family, are not based on what you can give in financial terms. Family is rooted in love, care, and mutual respect, transcending superficial material gain. A caring family loves you for who you are, not for what you have.

Unconditional love means that family members stand by each other without expecting anything in return. They celebrate your victories and support you during your lowest points. The love of a parent for their child, or the bond between siblings, cannot be equated to any material possessions. This deep-rooted connection offers security that is far more lasting than the fleeting comfort money can bring. While money can fluctuate, the love of a close-knit family is a constant, grounding force.

## 3. Shared Experiences and Memories

While wealth can enable people to create lavish experiences, the most meaningful moments in life often come from shared experiences with loved ones, not from material possessions. The time spent together—during holidays, family gatherings, or even in everyday life—creates memories that are far more precious than any material gift. These shared experiences shape who we are and offer a sense of belonging and continuity.

As life progresses, material possessions may lose their value, but memories of family endure. A simple dinner at home with loved ones, a heartfelt conversation, or a laugh shared among family members has a lasting emotional impact. These experiences form the essence of human life and are the moments we look back on with fondness in old age. Money cannot create these moments of genuine connection; they are fostered through the bonds of family.

## 4. Moral and Ethical Foundation

Family plays a significant role in shaping our values, beliefs, and sense of ethics. Money can provide education and opportunities, but the moral and ethical foundation that guides an individual's actions often comes from the teachings and values instilled by family. A caring family teaches us the importance of kindness, compassion, responsibility, and empathy. These lessons are invaluable in navigating life and building meaningful relationships outside the family circle.

Without a strong moral compass, one may lose direction, even if they have material wealth. Family provides the grounding necessary to ensure that we lead a fulfilling and ethical life. The lessons learned from a supportive family form the basis for personal integrity, and this is far more enduring than any financial success.

## 5. Longevity of Relationships

Money and material wealth are transient; they can be gained and lost over time. Family relationships, however, are lifelong. When nurtured with love, care, and respect, these relationships can last for generations, providing a sense of continuity that extends beyond the individual. While financial status may fluctuate, the bond of family remains consistent, offering a sense of stability and permanence that money cannot.

Family members grow old together, share life milestones, and witness each other's personal journeys. These relationships are deeply intertwined with our sense of identity and belonging. While wealth can offer temporary satisfaction, it cannot fill the void of loneliness or isolation that comes from lacking close, caring relationships. A family that truly cares about each other is a lifetime companion, one that cannot be replaced by financial means.

## 6. Support During Hard Times

Money can solve many practical problems, but it cannot heal a broken heart, ease the pain of loss, or give comfort during personal struggles. A caring family provides the kind of support that no financial resource can. In times of illness, for instance, family members are often the ones who offer care and companionship, far beyond what money can buy. Their presence brings comfort and healing, making even the toughest situations bearable.

In situations where finances are tight, it is the family's support that keeps individuals going. Families pool together their resources, be they financial, emotional, or practical, to help one another through difficult times. This collective strength is irreplaceable and proves time and again that family is the ultimate support system, especially in times of need.

## 7. The Importance of Legacy

Wealth is something that can be passed down to future generations, but the legacy of a family is much richer than financial inheritance. A family's legacy is its traditions, its values, its stories, and its love. These are the things that last far beyond the accumulation of wealth. The connections, morals, and memories passed down through generations are what truly enrich the lives of descendants. A caring family leaves behind a legacy of love, kindness, and togetherness, which holds far more significance than any material inheritance.

A family that nurtures its relationships will leave behind a legacy that inspires future generations. This legacy of love and togetherness will ripple through time, shaping future lives in ways that money could never accomplish.

## Conclusion

While money is important for comfort, security, and providing for one's needs, it pales in comparison to the importance of family. A caring family provides emotional support, unconditional love, a sense of belonging, and a moral foundation that money can never replicate. They are there through life's ups and downs, providing a safety net of love and understanding. Family is not just important; it is essential for a fulfilling and meaningful life. True wealth is not measured by the money in the bank, but by the strength and love of the family who stand by your side through it all.

Before anything else, building a good and supportive family should be one of life's most fundamental goals. A caring, respectful, and supportive family doesn't happen by chance; it is a product of conscious and loving parenting. The values of respect, care, and love are cultivated first within the family, primarily through how parents guide, nurture, and care for their children. The family unit serves as the foundation for the development of strong character, and it is where one learns to value relationships, practice empathy, and develop a moral compass.

# Parenting: The Key to a Strong Family

Good parenting is at the heart of creating a supportive and harmonious family. It is through parenting that the seeds of love, respect, and responsibility are planted. A parent's role is not just to provide for their child's material needs, but to mold their character, instill values, and prepare them for the world. Children learn how to navigate life through the examples set by their parents. When parents model respect, kindness, and compassion, children are more likely to carry these traits into adulthood, which is critical for creating a healthy family dynamic.

One of the most important lessons that parents can impart is respect. Respect for parents, elders, and for one another forms the basis of all healthy relationships. A family that operates on mutual respect creates an environment where all members feel valued, heard, and supported. Teaching children to respect their parents sets the tone for how they will approach other relationships in life, as well as how they will later approach their own parenting roles.

## Respect for Parents: The Cornerstone of Family

In many cultures, respecting one's parents is seen as not only a virtue but a duty. Parents are the first teachers and the ones who sacrifice to ensure their children's well-being and growth. Believing in your parents, trusting in their guidance, and honoring them throughout life creates a bond that cannot be easily broken. This respect is the foundation of a strong family structure. When children believe in their parents as good people and respect them, they are more likely to listen to their advice, value their wisdom, and carry forward the family values.

Respect for parents also fosters a deep sense of gratitude and humility. Understanding the sacrifices made by parents helps children appreciate their upbringing and the efforts put into their personal development. This understanding translates into a deeper connection and a lifelong bond between parents and children, reinforcing the idea that family is not just a relationship of convenience, but a lifelong commitment to love and care.

## The Role of Character in Family Life

Developing good character is one of the primary goals of parenting. A family thrives when each member embodies positive character traits like honesty, kindness, responsibility, and empathy. Good character is not innate; it is shaped by the environment in which a child grows up. Parents play a vital role in nurturing these traits through their behavior, their words, and the values they uphold in everyday life.

Children who grow up in a family where love, respect, and support are abundant are more likely to develop into individuals who exhibit these same qualities in their own lives. This, in turn, strengthens the family unit because every member is contributing positively to the overall dynamic. The way a child is raised directly impacts their future relationships, including how they will one day treat their own family. When parents prioritize teaching their children to be good people above all else, they set the foundation for a caring and respectful family for generations to come.

## Belief in One's Family: A Source of Strength

Belief in one's family is crucial for creating a strong, united household. When family members trust and believe in each other, they form a cohesive unit that can withstand any challenges that come their way. Believing in your parents as good people helps to establish this trust early on. When children believe in their parents' wisdom and good intentions, they feel secure and confident in their upbringing. This belief strengthens the family bond and creates an atmosphere of mutual trust and respect.

A family that believes in each other is also better equipped to support one another in times of need. Whether facing personal struggles or external difficulties, family members who believe in each other's abilities and goodness can offer encouragement, advice, and emotional support. This sense of belief builds resilience within the family, allowing each member to face life's challenges with the confidence that they have a strong support system behind them.

## First make a Family as the Goal of Life. (All are Happy and pray for each other's success - No place for jealous)

In many ways, creating a caring, loving, and respectful family is the ultimate goal of life. Material success, while important, is secondary to the fulfillment and joy that comes from being part of a supportive family. The happiness that comes from knowing you are surrounded by people who love and care for you unconditionally cannot be replaced by any material wealth. Raising children to be good, caring, and respectful individuals ensures that the cycle of love and support continues across generations.

Life is full of uncertainties, but family is a constant source of strength and comfort. When children are raised in an environment that prioritizes love, respect, and moral values, they grow up with the tools necessary to lead fulfilling lives. More importantly, they carry forward these lessons into their own families, creating a ripple effect that positively impacts the world around them.

Before we chase after wealth, fame, or success, the most important thing we can do is focus on building a good, supportive, and caring family. This starts with effective parenting, where children are taught the values of respect, kindness, and empathy. Respecting parents and believing in their goodness fosters a deep bond that serves as the cornerstone of family life. In the end, the goal of life is not just to accumulate material wealth, but to create a loving family where all members support, care for, and believe in each other. A strong family is life's greatest treasure, offering a wealth of love, care, and respect that no amount of money can buy.

A family plagued by jealousy is like a boat with holes in the middle of the ocean, slowly sinking as the water seeps in. Jealousy, when allowed to fester within a family, undermines the core values of love, trust, and unity that hold the family together. Instead of supporting one another and celebrating each other's successes, family members become consumed by envy and resentment. This toxic environment creates emotional distance and fuels a destructive cycle, where every small victory is met with bitterness instead of joy. Just like a boat in the ocean, the family may seem to stay afloat at first, but over time, the damage caused by jealousy will lead to irreparable loss.

As jealousy takes root, the first casualty is respect. In a family, respect is essential for harmony and cooperation, but jealousy erodes it. When one member of the family is constantly comparing themselves to another or feeling envious of their achievements, they begin to lose respect for that person. Conversations become laced with passive-aggressive remarks, and small arguments escalate into bigger conflicts. Over time, this lack of respect spreads like wildfire, infecting the entire family dynamic. The mutual admiration and trust that once held the family together start to crumble, making it impossible for members to function as a supportive unit.

Beyond respect, jealousy can also impact a family's financial and emotional well-being. A family that competes with each other rather than working together may end up making unwise financial decisions out of spite. For example, a sibling might overspend in an attempt to "outshine" another, or parents might unfairly favor one child financially, fueling more jealousy and resentment. These kinds of decisions drain resources and create financial instability, leading to losses that could have been avoided if the family had worked as a team instead of being divided by jealousy. Money problems, often caused by internal competition and unfair treatment, add another layer of tension to the already fragile relationships.

Perhaps the greatest loss in a jealous family is the impact it has on the children. Kids are highly perceptive, and they learn from the environment they grow up in. When they see their parents or other family members constantly comparing, competing, and resenting each other, they internalize these behaviors. This not only creates a toxic home environment, but it also teaches children to view relationships through the lens of competition and envy, rather than love and cooperation. As a result, they may struggle to form healthy, trusting relationships in the future, carrying the legacy of jealousy into their own lives. In essence, jealousy in the family can corrupt the next generation, passing down a cycle of mistrust and emotional instability.

Ultimately, jealousy within a family is a manifestation of the natural law that "what you give is what you get." A family that nurtures jealousy will only reap more division, loss, and emotional pain. Just like a boat with holes in the ocean, a family that is fractured by jealousy will slowly lose everything—respect, money, and even the emotional bonds that hold them together. However, a family that works to replace jealousy with love, support, and encouragement will experience the opposite: a strong, resilient unit that can withstand life's storms. In the end, the choice lies with each family member—what they give to the family is exactly what they will get back.

A heartwarming book! "Mother is Heaven and Father is way of Heaven" by Nadeem Pasha emphasizes the significance of parents in our lives. By highlighting their importance, the book aims to promote family values and respect for one's parents.

www.ingramcontent.com/pod-product-compliance
Lightning Source LLC
LaVergne TN
LVHW061559070526
838199LV00077B/7112